Arielle

PARIS,
FRACE ♡

Seven Wonders of
ARCHITECTURE

Ann Kerns

TWENTY-FIRST CENTURY BOOKS

Minneapolis

Twenty-First Century Books
A division of Lerner Publishing Group, Inc.
241 First Avenue North
Minneapolis, MN 55401 U.S.A.

Website address: www.lernerbooks.com

Library of Congress Cataloging-in-Publication Data

Kerns, Ann, 1959–
    Seven wonders of architecture / by Ann Kerns.
    p.   cm. — (Seven wonders)
    Includes bibliographical references and index.
    ISBN 978–0–7613–4236–6 (lib. bdg. : alk. paper)
    1. Architecture, Modern—Juvenile literature. 2. Architecture—Miscellanea—Juvenile literature. I. Title.
    NA500.K47 2010
    720—dc22   2009006183

Manufactured in the United States of America
1 – DP – 12/15/09

Contents

Introduction ——— 4

1 Saint Peter's Basilica ——— 7

2 The Taj Mahal ——— 17

3 The Eiffel Tower ——— 27

4 The Sears Tower ——— 37

5 The Sydney Opera House ——— 47

6 Burj al Arab ——— 57

7 Taipei 101 ——— 65

Timeline ——— 72
Choose an Eighth Wonder ——— 73
Glossary ——— 74
Source Notes ——— 75
Selected Bibliography ——— 76
Further Reading and Websites ——— 76
Index ——— 78

INTRODUCTION

*P*EOPLE LOVE TO MAKE LISTS OF THE BIGGEST AND THE BEST. ALMOST TWENTY-FIVE HUNDRED YEARS AGO, A GREEK WRITER NAMED HERODOTUS MADE A LIST OF THE MOST AWESOME THINGS EVER BUILT BY PEOPLE. THE LIST INCLUDED BUILDINGS, STATUES, AND OTHER OBJECTS THAT WERE LARGE AND IMPRESSIVE. LATER, OTHER WRITERS ADDED NEW ITEMS TO THE LIST. WRITERS EVENTUALLY AGREED ON A FINAL LIST. IT WAS CALLED THE SEVEN WONDERS OF THE ANCIENT WORLD.

The list became famous, and people began imitating it. They made other lists of wonders. They listed the Seven Wonders of the Modern World and the Seven Wonders of the Middle Ages. People even made lists of undersea wonders.

They also made lists of architectural wonders. Architecture is the design of buildings. People create buildings for many reasons. They use them for housing and for religious worship. They can be places to earn money and trade goods and places to meet for fun and entertainment. The simplest family house and the grandest government building are parts of the field of architecture.

Architecture is a very old field. In ancient Asia, India, Greece, and Rome, people created buildings according to their ideas of what was beautiful, elegant, and useful. Modern cultures use those ideas and designs too. But people's needs shift. Ideas of what is useful and beautiful change. We discover new materials and new technology (practical uses for scientific discoveries). And we develop new construction (building) techniques. Architecture of the modern period has its roots in the past, but it is always changing.

A WONDERFUL ADVENTURE

How buildings are used is an important part of architecture. Many buildings also become famous for the way they look, their size, or their amazing features. They can even become symbols of a culture or a time period. This book explores seven wonders of architecture that are amazing in all these ways.

One of the first stops on our tour of the modern world of architecture is a grand monument to a queen. We will also visit an iron tower that became a symbol of a city. Two different buildings are designed to look like the sails of a boat. These and other fascinating places are waiting. Read on to begin your adventure.

Travelers to India spread the word of the wondrous Taj Mahal from as early as the 1700s.

1 Saint Peter's BASILICA

Saint Peter's Basilica stands near the bank of the Tiber River in Rome, Italy. The building's official name, in Italian, is Basilica Papale di San Pietro in Vaticano.

$\mathcal{V}$ISITORS TO ROME, ITALY, NEVER FIND THEMSELVES SHORT OF THINGS TO SEE AND DO. ROME HAS BEEN A CITY FOR MORE THAN TWO THOUSAND YEARS. ANCIENT RUINS LIE AMID THE CITY'S HISTORIC HILLS. MEDIEVAL PALACES AND CHURCHES OVERLOOK BUSTLING PIAZZAS (PUBLIC SQUARES). THE WATER IN FOUNTAINS SPARKLES IN THE SUN.

Rome is also home to the Vatican City. The Vatican City is a tiny, independent state within the city of Rome. It is the center of the Roman Catholic Church. The leader of the church, the pope, lives in the Vatican. Many visitors from all over the world come to see the Vatican's buildings and art treasures. Among those buildings is Saint Peter's Basilica. The basilica is Rome's most famous church. It is the largest Christian church in the world.

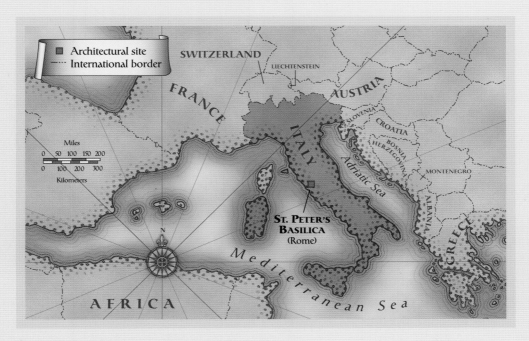

A Sacred Site

Saint Peter's Basilica took almost two centuries to plan and build, beginning in the 1400s. Its history involves twenty-seven popes and many architects. The basilica was built on one of the most sacred (holy) sites in the Christian world. In Christian tradition, it is the burial place of Saint Peter.

Peter was one of the twelve apostles, the close companions of Jesus Christ. After Jesus's death about A.D. 36, Peter became the leader of Christianity. This was the name of the new religion based on the teachings of Jesus. According to tradition, Peter traveled to Rome to preach Christianity.

In the first century A.D., Rome was an empire—a large group of lands ruled by one central leader. It had its own religion, which was a very important part of Roman culture and politics. As Christianity began to attract followers, Roman leaders saw the new religion as a threat. They began to imprison and execute Christians. In A.D. 64, the Roman emperor Nero ordered the execution of Peter. After Peter's death, his followers buried him near the Circus of Nero, a public gathering place in northwest Rome.

Early Christians built a small shrine over Peter's grave. Then, in A.D. 326, Emperor Constantine ordered the construction of a church on the site. Constantine was Rome's first Christian emperor. His church was a basilica, a large church that held special ceremonies.

Roman Ruins

In the 400s, the western part of the Roman Empire collapsed. As the empire faded, the Roman Catholic Church grew. Over the centuries, it became the most powerful institution in Europe. Rome became its religious and cultural center.

This bronze panel shows Peter holding two keys, symbols of his leadership of the Christian religion. Made in the mid-1400s, the panel decorated the central door of the first Saint Peter's Basilica.

Italian artist Domenico Tasselli made this picture of the interior of the first Saint Peter's Basilica in the late 1500s. The basilica was more than ten stories tall at its highest point.

But in 1309, Pope Clement V decided to move the papacy (the center of the Catholic Church) to Avignon, France. All the clergy, teachers, visitors, artists, and architects moved away too. Rome began to decay quickly. Buildings began to crumble. Wild animals roamed the streets.

Pope Gregory XI moved the papacy back to Rome in 1376. The church began rebuilding the city, often using stones from ancient Roman buildings. The Basilica of Saint Peter was in bad shape, and the church made plans to restore it. But the basilica's walls were leaning badly. People feared the whole building would fall over. By the 1400s, the church was discussing whether the eleven-hundred-year-old basilica needed to be completely replaced.

In 1505 Pope Julius II announced plans to tear down the basilica and build a new one. Julius was a strong and ambitious leader with a larger-than-life personality. He wanted to build a basilica that would be the greatest church in the Christian world. It would make Rome the glory of Europe.

Many Roman Catholics did not share the pope's enthusiasm for the project. In fact, they were outraged at the idea of tearing down the old basilica. It was an ancient and sacred building. Julius went ahead with his plans. But to avoid argument, he planned to begin building the new basilica directly behind the old church.

BRAMANTE'S VISION

The 1500s were part of the Renaissance, a historical period that began in Europe in the early 1400s. Renaissance thinkers, teachers, and artists greatly admired the art, architecture, and writings of ancient Greece and Rome.

The Renaissance was especially strong on the Italian Peninsula. The Roman Empire had been centered in Italy. Roman statues, arches, temples, domes, and columns could still be found in Italian cities. Renaissance architects studied those structures to understand Roman design and construction. One of the architects was Donato Bramante (1444–1514). In October 1505, Julius II hired Bramante to design the new basilica.

Bramante shared Julius's vision of the basilica as a huge and magnificent building. The architect based his design on two ancient Roman buildings—the Basilica of Maxentius and the Pantheon. The Roman basilica was a public hall where people gathered. The Pantheon was a domed temple (place of worship) built for the Roman gods.

The new basilica would have a large, open interior. It would be crowned by a round dome. For the basic shape of the building, Bramante chose a Greek cross. The cross is an important Christian symbol, and there are many varieties of cross shapes. A Greek cross has two bars of equal length, which cross in the center. The center of this cross would sit directly over the burial place of Saint Peter.

In Rome, Bramante (above) was famous for building the Tempietto (below) in 1502. Bramante modeled the Tempietto after Roman temples. It has a circular dome and a row of Greek-style columns. The small building marks the spot where Saint Peter was executed.

BUILDING BEGINS

Bramante had his vision. But he still had to make practical plans for building it. He especially had to figure out how to support the basilica's huge, heavy dome. Bramante turned again to the ancient Romans.

The Romans constructed many buildings, roadways, and other projects. Along the way, they developed concrete. Concrete is a mixture of sand, crushed rocks, and water. Concrete is much lighter than stone or brick. And when it's wet, it can be poured into shapes. It then dries very hard and strong. The ancient Romans had used concrete to build their domes. Bramante would make the basilica's dome out of concrete. It would be light enough to be held up by four legs, or piers.

Bramante also planned to use concrete to form the basilica's ceilings. The ceilings would be rounded, like a series of connected arches. In architecture this is called a vaulted ceiling. Like the dome, the concrete ceiling would be lighter than a stone or brick ceiling. Bramante would not need a lot of walls and columns inside to support the ceiling. That would allow for open spaces inside the church.

In the late fall of 1505, Bramante's workers began digging the foundation behind the old basilica. Once the foundation stones were laid, workers began

The Basilica of Maxentius in Rome was one of the largest buildings built by the ancient Romans. Many of its walls are made of concrete.

building the first pier. The four piers would support the dome. They would form the central interior square of the basilica. Each arm of the cross would be built out from a side of that square.

Bramante also began to tear down the old basilica. He did not order workers to remove the contents of the church before they began. They destroyed ancient artwork and altars. Angry Romans demanded that they stop. After that, Bramante was careful to tear down the old basilica in sections.

PLANS CHANGE

By the spring of 1507, the first pier was finished. It stood 90 feet (27 meters) tall and measured 232 feet (71 m) around. Workers moved quickly to finish the other piers. Meanwhile, Julius worked on raising money for the project. As construction costs mounted, he asked many wealthy Italians and European royalty to contribute funds.

In 1512 Julius died without ever even seeing the dome on his grand basilica. Two years later, Bramante died. For the next thirty years, construction went ahead very slowly. New popes were elected. Architects, too, came and went. They changed the design and added their own ideas. During this time, the Vatican struggled to pay for the enormous church. Catholics in other parts of Europe argued that they should not have to pay for the Vatican's architectural projects.

A Dutch artist sketched this picture of the new Saint Peter's Basilica under construction in the ruins of the old basilica in the 1530s.

Two Artists

Some of Italy's best artists, architects, and artisans (skilled workers such as stone carvers) worked on Saint Peter's Basilica. Among the most famous were Michelangelo (1475–1564) and Raphael Sanzio (1483–1520). Both artists had worked in the Vatican for many years before they took over as basilica architects. Raphael had painted much of the artwork in Julius II's living quarters. At the same time, Michelangelo had painted the ceiling of the Sistine Chapel. This is a small church near Saint Peter's.

Both Michelangelo and Raphael were talented artists. Both worked in the Vatican. But they led very different lives. Raphael was young and handsome. He was very popular in Roman society and had many friends. Michelangelo preferred to be alone. He would often lock even Pope Julius II out of the Sistine Chapel so that he could work in silence. He would be so absorbed in his art that he would forget to eat and bathe. Raphael died young after a short illness. Michelangelo lived into old age.

THE DOME RISES

In 1547 Michelangelo Buonarroti (1475–1564) took over the basilica project. Although he was seventy-two, he was still the most famous artist in Italy. Under his direction, construction of the dome finally began. Michelangelo built the dome's base, called the drum. It was 65 feet (20 m) tall and 600 feet (183 m) in diameter. He surrounded the drum with sixteen columns.

After Michelangelo's death, Giacomo della Porta (ca. 1533–1602) took over the basilica project. He, too, focused his work on the dome. He changed the shape slightly and created a new construction plan. Workers spent twenty-two months raising the dome. It was finished on May 14, 1590. The dome rises 448 feet (137 m) above the floor of the basilica.

Della Porta added a lantern (a small round tower) at the peak of the dome. In 1593 a copper ball and bronze cross were added to the lantern. The ball is 8 feet (2.4 m) in diameter and weighs 5,493 pounds (2,492 kilograms). The cross is 16 feet (5 m) tall.

In 1608 the last of the old basilica was torn down. This made room for the new basilica's nave and facade (front). The new architect, Carlo Moderno, decided to use the Latin cross (a cross shaped like a t, with one bar longer than the other) as the layout of the basilica. With a Latin cross design, the nave would be longer and would hold larger crowds. When finished, the nave measured 613 feet (187 m) long, 84 feet (26 m) wide, and 152 feet (46 m) high.

Moderno built the facade 375 feet (114 m) wide and 167 feet (51 m) high. At the very front, he built a portico, a large covered porch. The portico serves as the entrance to the basilica. In the center of the portico is the Benediction Balcony. It was built so that the pope could greet the crowds that gather outside Saint Peter's. The portico was finished in 1612.

THE INTERIOR

Inside the basilica, artists decorated the walls, ceilings, and columns. Marble, gilt (a thin layer of gold), and mosaic (tiny pieces of colored stone laid in patterns) cover the interior. The walls are lined with enormous sculptures of Catholic saints and popes. A marble staircase leads to the underground tomb of Saint Peter.

An altar stands directly beneath the dome and above the tomb. Around the altar is a bronze structure called the Baldacchino. It was built by the artist Gianlorenzo Bernini (1598–1680). The Baldacchino is 98 feet (30 m) tall. Its four columns are twisted and carved to look like the stems and leaves of plants.

THE PIAZZA

After construction of the basilica was complete, Bernini began plans to build a piazza in front. He designed two curving colonnades—covered passageways lined with columns. The colonnades formed an oval. One end was left open as an entrance. Work on the piazza began in August 1657 and was done in 1667.

Elaborate decorations cover the walls and ceilings inside Saint Peter's Basilica. The twisted columns of the Baldacchino stand beneath the dome.

This picture shows the piazza as viewed from the roof of Saint Peter's Basilica.

The piazza measures 1,115 feet (340 m) long by 650 feet (198 m) wide. The colonnades contain three hundred columns. Along the top of the colonnades are 164 statues of saints and popes. Each statue is about 12 feet (4 m) tall and took two months to carve.

In Italian the piazza is called the Piazza San Pietro. In English it is known as Saint Peter's Square. In modern Rome, a street called the Via della Conciliazione leads to the square. More than four million tourists each year cross Saint Peter's Square to see the basilica. The church is open every day. Visitors can even climb the 320 steps of the dome to reach the very peak of this architectural wonder.

"St Peter's Basilica is the reason why Rome is still the center of the civilized world. For religious, historical, and architectural reasons it by itself justifies a journey to Rome."
—Helen F. North, classics professor, quoted in City Secrets: Rome, 1999

Saint Peter's Basilica

15

THE
Taj Mahal

Built in the 1600s, the Taj Mahal is one of India's national treasures. The four kiosks on the roof of the main building are called chhatris. *The arched entryways are called* pishtaqs.

$\mathcal{I}$N THE LATE 1700S, BRITISH VISITORS TO INDIA RETURNED WITH SOME AMAZING TALES. ONE TALE TOLD OF A SHIMMERING WHITE BUILDING TOPPED WITH A HUGE DOME. IT WAS SURROUNDED BY GARDENS AND FOUNTAINS. THIS AMAZING STRUCTURE, TRAVELERS SAID, WAS BUILT AS A MONUMENT TO LOVE. INSIDE THE BUILDING, UNDER THE ENORMOUS DOME, WAS THE TOMB OF A QUEEN. HER HUSBAND WAS HEARTBROKEN AT HER SUDDEN DEATH. HE BUILT THE MONUMENT IN HER HONOR.

Tales of this building, the Taj Mahal, were true. It was built as a tomb for the beloved wife of an Indian ruler. And it still stands as India's most famous and beautiful building.

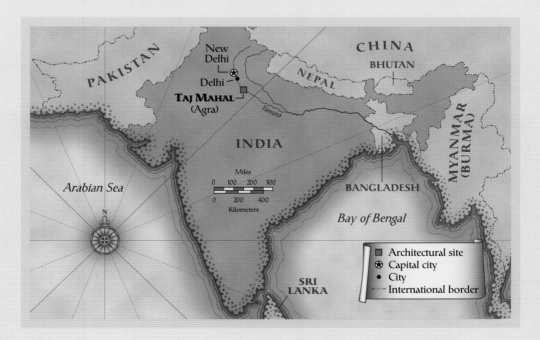

THE MUGHAL EMPIRE

Nice culture [handwritten annotation]

India is an ancient land with a long history of art, literature, architecture, and religion. Centuries ago, large parts of India were ruled by the Mughals. The Mughals were Muslims who came to India from central Asia. They made Agra, in north central India, their capital city. *Good informatio* [handwritten annotation]

The Mughals had their own traditions of art, architecture, and religion. They also admired Indian art and tradition. By blending the two cultures, the Mughals hoped to show themselves as the rightful rulers of India.

In 1592 a Mughal prince named Khurram was born. From childhood, Khurram trained to be a Mughal emperor. He learned sword fighting and horseback riding. He studied religion, art, poetry and, one his favorite subjects—architecture. *Cool, why those subjects?* [handwritten annotation]

As a young man, Khurram was given the name Shah Jahan (king of the world). In 1611 he married the first of his three wives. All his wives were treated well as royal princesses. But Shah Jahan fell deeply in love with his second wife. She was the beautiful and kind Arjumand Banu Begum. He called her Mumtaz Mahal—the chosen one of the palace. *How was he king of the world?* [handwritten annotation]

Shah Jahan became the Mughal emperor in 1628. He used his interest in art and architecture to display the empire's strength and wealth. He built many beautiful palaces, houses, tombs for royal relatives, and formal gardens.

This pair of portraits shows Mumtaz Mahal (left) and Shah Jahan (right). The paintings come from a Persian book made sometime after 1666.

What else was being built about the same time as the Taj Mahal? The 1600s was a busy building time in many parts of the world.

1616: English architect Inigo Jones started building the Queen's House in Greenwich, England, for Queen Ann, wife of King James I.

1620: Pilgrims in the American colonies built the common house of the Plimoth Plantation in Massachusetts.

1620: The Imperial Villa was built in Katsura, Japan.

1630: Construction began on the Great Synagogue (Jewish house of worship) of Vilna in Lithuania.

1632: King Louis XIII of France built a hunting lodge outside Paris—a building that grew to become the Palace of Versailles.

1642: Building began on the Potala Palace, a retreat for the leader of Tibet, in Lhasa, Tibet.

1657: Italian architect Gianlorenzo Bernini began building Saint Peter's Square in Rome.

1675: English architect Christopher Wren began work on Saint Paul's Cathedral in London, England.

THE EMPEROR'S GRIEF

On June 16, 1631, Mumtaz Mahal died after giving birth to her fourteenth child. Shah Jahan was heartbroken. He refused to appear in public. He thought about giving up his throne and going to live alone.

But even in his grief, Shah Jahan began plans for a magnificent tomb, the Taj Mahal. It would sit in a peaceful garden on the banks of the Yamuna River in Agra. It would have a beautiful dome that shone in the sunlight and glowed in the moonlight. The tomb would represent paradise—the new home of his beloved queen.

CONSTRUCTION BEGINS

Construction began in January 1632. Shah Jahan met with his team of architects every day. The architects did not make written plans. The chief architect drew the plans in chalk on the ground. Other architects and work supervisors studied the plans to know how to go ahead with construction.

The plans followed some of the basic rules of Mughal and Islamic architecture. Both styles used symbols and matching shapes (such as only one style of column). Also very important was symmetry—matching elements in building and decoration. The Taj complex

The Taj Mahal

Indian stone carvers use traditional tools to carve red sandstone panels outside the Taj Mahal during a 2004 restoration of the complex.

was built south to north toward the river. The project started with the simplest public areas. These lead toward the domed mausoleum (the building that held the tomb).

Shah Jahan ordered red sandstone, a soft rock, from quarries (rock mines) 25 miles (40 km) west of Agra. He ordered white marble from quarries 250 miles (400 km) away. Both were hauled to Agra on carts pulled by water buffalo. Bricks were made right at the site in Agra.

Shah Jahan also brought in skilled stone cutters, carvers, and bricklayers from all over India. Historians say that more than one thousand workers were on the construction site every day.

"In this peaceful reign the work of building has reached such a point that it astonishes even the world traveler."

—*Lahauri, Shah Jahan's chief historian, 1600s*

The Taj Complex

At the south end of the site, workers began building the market quarter. Two cross streets formed the bazaar, a group of small shops. At the four corners of the market, they built caravanserais. A caravanserai is an inn for travelers.

The south gate separates the market quarter from the next section, the forecourt. The forecourt also has gates on its east and west sides. Visitors to Mumtaz Mahal's tomb could enter through those gates and dismount their horses and elephants. The forecourt gave them a space to prepare to enter the more sacred and peaceful parts of the complex.

From the forecourt, visitors passed through the gate. The great gate is made of sandstone trimmed in white marble. The main entrance is through a pointed arch. At each corner of the gate is an eight-sided tower topped by a small dome.

On the other side of the great gate, workers prepared the garden. A long, narrow pool with fountains runs through the center of the garden. Workers also began planting trees so that the trees would be grown by the time the Taj Mahal was finished.

The Mausoleum

At the north end of the garden, workers built a flat base for the mausoleum. It had to be strong. The domed mausoleum and two other buildings would sit on it. The site was close to the river, and the ground was covered in sand and

Elaborate decorations cover the walls of the great gate of the Taj Mahal.

loose soil. Workers had to dig down until they hit hard ground on which they could build.

When the platform was done, builders began the mausoleum. As the most important building in the complex, it is made of the most expensive materials. Workers first built the walls with bricks and mortar. Mortar, when it hardens, holds bricks together. Once the walls were complete, they were faced with, or covered in, sheets of white marble. The heavy white marble was held in place with iron pins and clamps.

Workers then built the tomb's domes. They built a large central dome surrounded by four smaller domes. Like the walls, the domes were built of bricks faced with white marble.

The workers built identical buildings on either side of the tomb. To the west is the Taj mosque, a Muslim place of worship. To the east is the matching *mihman khana*. This hall was used for important visitors and for celebrations in memory of Mumtaz Mahal. At each corner of the tomb platform is a minaret. This tall, thin tower is used in Muslim sacred rites.

The mausoleum is the building central to the Taj Mahal. It contains Mumtaz Mahal's burial chamber.

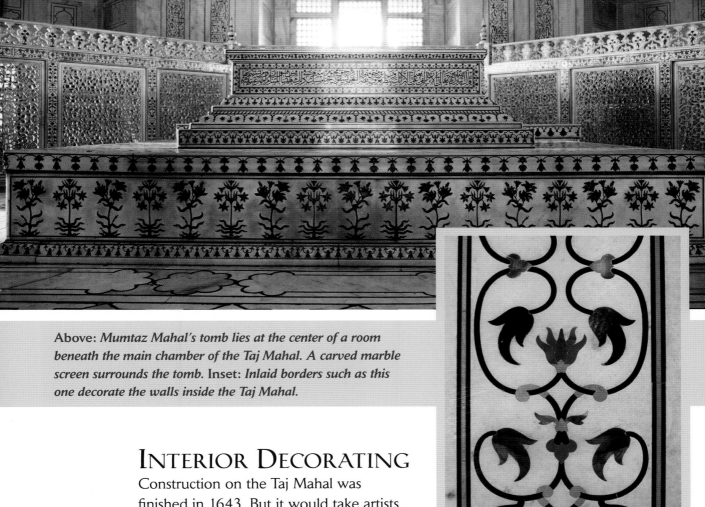

Above: *Mumtaz Mahal's tomb lies at the center of a room beneath the main chamber of the Taj Mahal. A carved marble screen surrounds the tomb.* Inset: *Inlaid borders such as this one decorate the walls inside the Taj Mahal.*

INTERIOR DECORATING

Construction on the Taj Mahal was finished in 1643. But it would take artists and artisans another five years to finish decorating the main buildings.

On the great gate, artists finished the pointed arch with inlaid marble. Inlay is a decorating method. A pattern is carved into a flat piece of material, such as marble. In this carved pattern, artists lay thin slices of colored stone to form a picture. Jade (a green stone), carnelian (a red stone), and lapis lazuli (a blue stone) are often used. The inlay patterns on the great gate are flowers and vines. The use of plants and other natural elements is common in Indian and Islamic decoration.

Inside the mausoleum is the tomb chamber. Here, workers covered Mumtaz Mahal's entire tomb with inlay flowers. Calligraphers carved the

"In all possible lights, from that of the full moon at midnight in a cloudless sky to that of the noonday sun, the mind seems to repose [rest]."
—Captain William Sleeman, a British official, describing the Taj Mahal in 1836

doorways with passages from the Quran (Islam's holy book). Shah Jahan ordered a sheet woven of pearls to lie on top of Mumtaz Mahal's tomb.

Outside, workers planted gardens. Historians are not sure exactly what was planted in the Taj garden. But they know that in India's hot climate, gardens were designed to be cool and fragrant. Most were filled with fruit, almond, and other flowering trees. Beds of herbs, roses, carnations, and poppies lined the paths. Workers also planted straight rows of cypress trees alongside the main walkways. They filled the pools and turned on the fountains.

A Place to Gather

The Taj Mahal became a center of activity in Agra. In the market quarter, shops sold medicine, food, perfumes, jewels, and silk. Traveling merchants stayed at the caravanserais while doing business at the bazaar. There was even room for the merchants' camels and horses.

At night, visitors enjoyed the gardens in the cooling air. The garden paths were lit with small lanterns. Water splashed in the fountains.

When Shah Jahan died in 1666, his tomb was placed next to Mumtaz Mahal's. It was also covered in inlay. The emperor and empress at last rested together.

In 1803 the British government gained control over the part of India that included Agra. British control made it easier for travelers from Europe to visit India. One of the most popular tourist sites was the beautiful Taj Mahal.

THE Black Taj

Mumtaz Mahal's tomb lies in the exact center of the tomb chamber. Shah Jahan's tomb is a little to the west. Some researchers believe that the shah did not plan to be buried at the Taj Mahal. They believe that shows that he meant to build his own mausoleum across the Yamuna River. It would be identical in shape to the Taj. But while the Taj is covered in white marble, the Shah's tomb was to be covered in black marble.

In the mid-1600s, a French traveler, Jean-Baptiste Tavernier, toured Agra. He claimed that he had seen workers digging the foundations for the Black Taj. If Shah Jahan was building his own tomb, he might have died before plans got very far.

THE MODERN TAJ MAHAL

In 1947 British rule in India ended. The Archaeological Survey of India took control of such sites as the Taj Mahal. The survey continues to take care of the Taj.

Into the 2000s, more than ten thousand people every day (thirteen thousand on weekend days) visit the Taj Mahal. The crowds make new problems for the 360-year-old monument. They wear down the paving stones of the gardens and the marble floors. Visitors' breath and body heat can damage the marble inside the tomb chamber. But the site remains an important place for Indians and foreign visitors. The Indian government is looking for solutions. They want to stop the damage. But they don't want to turn away the people who come to see Mumtaz Mahal's beautiful monument.

Thousands of people crowd around the mosque at the Taj Mahal for the Islamic festival of Eid al-Fitr. The Indian government hopes to protect the monument without closing it.

3 THE Eiffel Tower

For centuries, builders have used arches to bear weight. The arch can bear great weight to support walls and roofs. Arches are a part of the Eiffel Tower's design, but its arches are only decorative. The whole weight of the tower is carried by its legs.

$\mathscr{P}$ARIS, FRANCE, IS HOME TO MANY FAMOUS BUILDINGS. NOTRE DAME DE PARIS IS A BEAUTIFUL TWELFTH-CENTURY CATHEDRAL. THE LOUVRE, ONCE A PALACE, IS A MUSEUM HOUSING SOME OF THE WORLD'S MOST PRECIOUS ART. THE PARIS OPERA HOUSE IS A CENTER FOR OPERA, BALLET, AND MUSIC PERFORMANCES.

One of Paris's most famous landmarks is the Eiffel Tower, completed in 1889. In its day, it was the tallest structure in the world. It is still the tallest in Paris. But this architectural wonder was not built for religious use, art, or entertainment. The Eiffel Tower was built to show the possibilities of new construction technology. In other words, the tower was built as a monument to tower building.

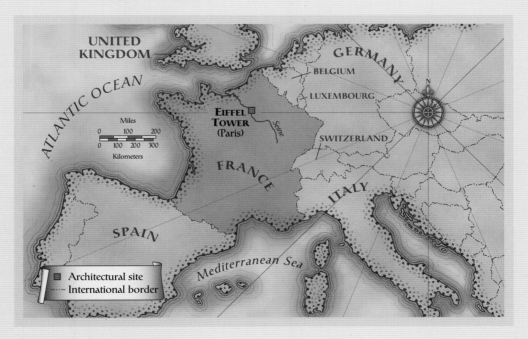

A New Age

For centuries people used their hands or simple tools to do daily work. But in Great Britain in the late 1700s, a big change took place. Inventors developed machines to do many kinds of work. Called the Industrial Revolution, this development spread through Europe and the United States in the 1800s.

Huge factories were built to quickly produce goods. Railroad systems—great highways made of iron—were laid to move those goods quickly and cheaply. As countries traded goods, the shipping industry boomed. Many mines were opened to provide coal and raw materials needed for the factories, trains, and ships.

The Industrial Revolution made many countries wealthy. In the 1870s, France discovered an iron mine near its eastern border. The mine helped France become a world power by 1880.

The country was eager to celebrate its success. France was approaching the one-hundredth anniversary of the French Revolution (1789–1799). During this historic event, the French king was overthrown. An elected government took his place. French leaders decided to combine the anniversary with an event that would celebrate the country's modern success. In November 1884, the French government announced that a world's fair would be held in Paris from May to October 1889. The fair would showcase industrial, scientific, and cultural achievements.

Eiffel's Tower

Government ministers wanted a big, impressive centerpiece for the fair. One popular suggestion was a tower that would stand about 1,000 feet (300 m) tall. No such tower had ever been built. In spring 1886, the government announced a contest for French architects and engineers. They had two months to submit their plans for the world's tallest structure.

Rejected Plans

After they announced their contest, exposition planners received more than one hundred tower blueprints (building plans). Some were better than others. Among the rejects was a plan for a tower built to be a giant lawn sprinkler. The designer claimed that the tower could be used to water Paris during dry spells. Another tower was designed in the form of a huge guillotine—a device used to behead people during the French Revolution. Exposition managers passed on that plan too.

During his long career, Gustave Eiffel designed bridges and buildings in many countries, including Chile, France, Turkey, Vietnam, and the Philippines.

Gustave Eiffel (1832–1923) was one step ahead of the government. Eiffel already had a team of architects and engineers working on plans for a tower. Eiffel was France's most respected engineer. He had designed and built bridges and railroad stations. As the country's rail system grew, Eiffel became a master designer of iron structures.

Eiffel believed that the tallest tower in the world could not be built of stone using old construction methods. The tower would be too heavy. Its foundation would sink, and its walls would crack. Eiffel had experience building bridges over mountain passes. He knew that winds are much stronger high above the earth. A very tall, solid tower would not be able to stand up to high winds.

Eiffel instead wanted a wrought iron tower with open walls. Wrought iron is a very strong and rigid type of iron. Eiffel thought it would make a perfect building material for his tower.

Maurice Koechlin, Eiffel and Company's chief engineer, designed the tower. The plan was submitted to the fair's managers and city leaders. The design was just what they had been hoping for. On January 8, 1887, Eiffel signed a contract to begin construction.

ON THE CHAMP DE MARS

The Eiffel Tower would be built on the Champ de Mars. The Champ de Mars is a field on the Left Bank of the Seine River in central Paris, where part of the fair was to be held. The tower would serve as a main entrance to the fair.

Eiffel took Koechlin's design and began to plan the construction. Eiffel measured, tested, and planned for every detail. He wanted a drawing of each piece of the tower. Fifty engineers and designers produced fifty-three hundred drawings of eighteen thousand items. The drawings used more than 14,000 square feet (1,300 sq. m) of paper.

> *"The tower to be erected at the Universal Exposition of 1889 should have a well-defined character and appear as an original masterpiece of the metals industry . . . and only the Eiffel Tower seemed to fulfill these requirements."*
>
> —*Universal Exposition contest subcommittee official record, June 1884*

Eiffel also began testing the ground under the Champs de Mars. Close to the river, the ground had a top layer of sand and gravel 20 feet (6 m) deep. Eiffel could not build on that, so he backed up from the river until he found solid ground. Workers broke ground (began digging) on January 26, 1887.

THE TOWER RISES

The base of the Eiffel Tower would form a square. Its side would measure 410 feet (125 m). At each corner would sit a four-sided pier that curved inward as it rose. The piers would bear the weight of the tower. To provide a foundation for the piers, Eiffel's workers dug down 33 feet (10 m) on the south and east sides and 49 feet (15 m) on the north and west.

Workers lay the foundation of the Eiffel Tower in 1887.

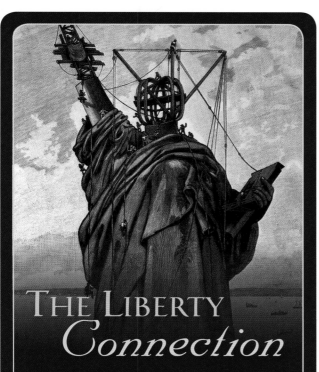

THE LIBERTY
Connection

In 1881 Auguste Bartholdi, a French sculptor, was working on an important project. Bartholdi had designed a giant statue. France was going to give it to the United States as a gesture of friendship. But Bartholdi was an artist, not an engineer. He needed help with the construction plans for such a large statue. In particular, Bartholdi was worried about the statue's right arm, which was to extend and hold a torch. He turned to Gustave Eiffel. Eiffel's company designed a strong iron frame for the statue, including the arm. An outer shell of copper would fit over the iron frame. The plan worked, and the Statue of Liberty *(above)* was built. It was unveiled in New York Harbor in 1886.

Workers poured 20 feet (6 m) of cement into each of the holes. They followed that with three layers of rock. Workers then drove an enormous anchor bolt—26 inches (66 centimeters) long—into the rock on each corner. They attached a piece of iron called a shoe to each bolt. Inside each shoe was a sliding piece of metal called a piston. The piston could be used to make adjustments to the height of the piers. After the pistons were installed, the base of each pier was attached to an iron shoe.

Work crews then began building the piers. Much of the work was prefabricated, or made ahead of time. Eiffel had a metal workshop in suburban Paris. Workers formed pieces in the shop. Then they sent them to the Champ de Mars site on horse-drawn wagons. At the tower site, steam-driven cranes lifted the pieces onto the structure. Workers used rivets (metal bolts) to secure the pieces in place.

NEW HEIGHTS

When the piers grew too high for the cranes on the ground, Eiffel installed creeper cranes. The creeper cranes "crept up" the structure by moving on rails inside the piers. The creeper cranes could turn in nearly a full circle to pick up and move metal beams. Visitors to the work site had never seen anything like it.

Above: *Cranes surround the Eiffel Tower during construction of the first platform.* Inset: *A viewer stands near one of the enormous trusses designed by Gustave Eiffel for the tower.*

At 187 feet (57 m), workers joined together the four piers with trussing. Trussing is a framework formed by bands or beams. This trussing supported the tower's first platform. It formed a base for the rest of the tower. The platform had to be perfectly horizontal or the tower would topple over as it rose. Eiffel adjusted each piston in the base until the platform was level. Then everything was riveted into place.

In July 1888, workers built the second platform at 380 feet (116 m). Above the second platform, the four uprights meet to form a single column. At 906 feet (276 m), the third floor was installed. The tower rose another 36 feet (11 m) for a total height of 1,024 feet (312 m).

A "Tragic *Lamppost*"

Most Parisians were excited that their city would be home to the world's tallest building. But not everyone was thrilled. In February 1887, forty-seven French artists, writers, and architects wrote a letter of strong protest against construction of the tower.

The letter was published in the Paris newspaper *Le Temps*. It complained that the tower would be out of character with the beautiful and ancient city. The letter described the tower as "dizzyingly ridiculous" and said it looked like a "gigantic black factory chimney." The writer Guy de Maupassant called Eiffel's structure a "giant and disgraceful skeleton." Léon Bloy, also a writer, called the tower "a tragic lamppost."

Some of the protesters grew to admire the Eiffel Tower after it was complete. But de Maupassant never did. According to a popular legend, de Maupassant often ate at one of the tower's restaurants. The writer reportedly said that being inside the tower was the only way he could avoid looking at it.

Eiffel and his engineers raise the French flag atop the Eiffel Tower to celebrate the end of construction.

MEET ME AT THE FAIR

By March 1889, construction was complete. Eiffel had built his wondrous tower on time and under budget. On March 31, Eiffel, two of his engineers, and a few officials climbed the tower's 1,710 stairs. Eiffel planted the French flag at the very top.

On May 6, the fair officially opened. The fairgrounds covered 228 acres (92 hectares). It spread across four areas of Paris—the Champ de Mars, the Esplanade des Invalides, the Quai d'Orsay, and the Trocadero gardens.

Visitors take in the view from the Eiffel Tower during the 1889 World's Fair. The tower served as the entrance gate to the fair.

Five hundred thousand people came to the fair the first day. In all, more than thirty-two million attended. Electric streetlights had just been installed in Paris, and this world's fair was the first one ever to be open at night. Fairgoers toured the grounds during the day. With the lights, they could stay on through the evening. Boats strung with lanterns cruised the Seine. Huge fountains glowed with colored lights. Fireworks lit the summer night skies.

The most popular attraction was the Eiffel Tower. During the first weeks of the fair, the tower was still without elevators. But that didn't stop anyone. Tens of thousands of people walked up the stairs to the first and second platforms. They ate at the tower's restaurants. They bought souvenirs and took in amazing views of the city. On a clear day, visitors could see up to 50 miles (80 km) away.

Almost two million people visited the Eiffel Tower during the fair—an average of eleven thousand a day.

Ever *Wonder?*

What does it take to keep the Eiffel Tower in shape? The tower is repainted every seven years. Repainting takes 66 tons (60 metric tons) of paint, twenty-five workers, and eighteen months. The platforms of the tower are cleaned daily. Over a year, that adds up to 4.4 tons (4 metric tons) of cleaning cloths, 106 gallons (400 liters) of detergent, and twenty-five thousand garbage bags. The tower's operating company also employs electricians, mechanics, plumbers, computer technicians, and metal workers. Tour guides, chefs, cooks, waitstaff, gift shop clerks, security guards, and office workers earn their living on the tower too.

Records show that people came from around the world. The first three names in the tower's guest book were tourists from Texas, Argentina, and Great Britain. Royalty and aristocracy from Great Britain, Greece, Italy, Russia, Egypt, and Siam (modern-day Thailand) also climbed the tower.

A MODERN MONUMENT

After the fair was over, Eiffel built a lab on the third platform to study the weather. Other scientists also used the tower for experiments. The use of radio signals for communications was growing. In the early 1900s, the tower was used as a giant radio antenna.

At night the Eiffel Tower glows with electrical lighting. In 2003 twenty-five mountain climbers worked to install a new lighting system in the tower.

Visitors continued to flock to the Eiffel Tower. It became a popular spot for tourists and a familiar site for Parisians. Over the years, it became a symbol of the city and one of the most familiar structures in the world.

In the 2000s, the Eiffel Tower still serves the communications industry. More than fifty television stations and thirty-one radio stations use the tower's 120 antennas. The antennas raise the tower's height to 1,063 feet (324 m).

About seven million people visit the Eiffel Tower every year. Historians estimate that one-quarter of a billion people have visited the tower in its lifetime. It remains a monument to the age of industry, a symbol of Paris, and a wonder of the architectural world.

4 THE Sears Tower

The Sears Tower rises above the other skyscrapers in Chicago's skyline. Its windows are tinted bronze, which shows when the sun is hitting the tower. But from a distance, the tower looks black.

CHICAGO, ILLINOIS, SITS ON THE WESTERN SHORE OF LAKE MICHIGAN. LAKE MICHIGAN'S COOL BLUE WATERS ARE POPULAR WITH BOATERS AND TOURISTS ON SIGHTSEEING CRUISES. FROM THE LAKE, BOATERS CAN SEE THE WHOLE CHICAGO SKYLINE. THE SKYLINE FEATURES SOME OF THE MOST BEAUTIFUL AND UNUSUAL BUILDINGS IN THE UNITED STATES. SOME OF THE BUILDINGS ARE OLD AND ORNATE (VERY DECORATED). SOME ARE SLEEK AND MODERN. RISING ABOVE THEM ALL IN THE CENTER OF THE SKYLINE IS A THIN BLACK TOWER. THIS IS CHICAGO'S MOST FAMOUS BUILDING—THE SEARS TOWER (RENAMED THE WILLIS TOWER IN 2009).

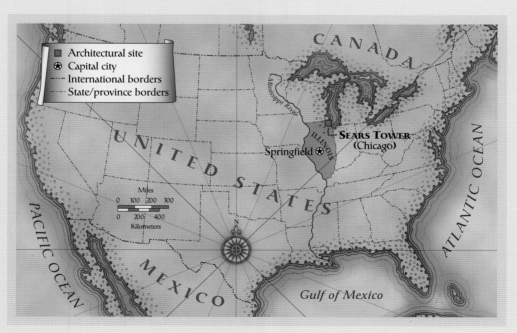

STEEL TOWERS

Built in 1973, the Sears Tower is a classic example of modern architecture. But its towering shape and smooth exterior have a long history. They are a part of the development of modern architectural design.

Throughout the nineteenth century, thousands of Americans moved from rural areas to cities such as Chicago. Many came to work in factories. Some found jobs in offices, stores, hotels, or restaurants. As the cities grew, neighborhoods became crowded. Open space was hard to come by. Architects realized that new buildings would have to rise up, not spread out.

In France in the late 1800s, Gustave Eiffel had built the tallest tower in the world out of wrought iron. The iron was strong, and it weighed much less than stone. In the United States, architects and engineers were experimenting with iron frames. Buildings could rise much higher if they were constructed around an iron frame rather than being built of solid stone walls.

Soon iron framing was replaced by steel. Steel is iron combined with other chemical elements such as carbon. The added chemicals make steel harder and stronger. Steel can also be heated and pulled, stretched, or shaped without breaking.

GOING *Up*

In the late 1800s, architects were eager to begin building skyscrapers. But before buildings got much taller, another invention had to be developed—the elevator. Elevators were used in the mid-1800s in mines and factories to move equipment and materials. But they weren't considered safe for people. Elisha Otis, a U.S. inventor, solved that problem in 1852. He designed a safety brake for elevator cars. If something went wrong with the elevator's system, the brake would stop the car from plunging down. The first passenger elevator was installed in a New York City department store in 1857.

Early elevators were powered by water pumps. The pumps took up a lot of space, and the elevators were very slow. In 1880 German engineer Werner von Siemens developed an electric elevator system. It was faster and more efficient than earlier systems. By the 1890s, electric elevators were being installed in U.S. skyscrapers.

SCRAPING THE SKY

In 1885 architect William Le Baron Jenney used steel framing to construct the Home Insurance Building in Chicago. At ten stories, it was the tallest office building in the world. People looking up at the building from the sidewalk called it a skyscraper. Within a decade, Chicago would have three more skyscrapers: the Tacoma Building (1889), the Masonic Temple (1892), and the Reliance Building (1895).

By the early twentieth century, Chicago was becoming famous for its buildings. Some of the most famous architects in the world were working in the city. The styles and new construction methods these architects used became known as the Chicago School.

Louis Sullivan (1856–1924) was a leader of the Chicago School. He worked on an architectural style known as modernism. Modernism began with new construction technology such as steel framing. A building's outside walls no longer needed columns, arches, and other supporting pieces. New buildings could have much simpler shapes and decoration. The new shapes would emphasize the vertical (the up and down direction).

THE MOVE DOWNTOWN

After World War II (1939–1945), Chicago became an important business center. Many of the buildings constructed in Chicago after the war were offices. Large companies such as Prudential Insurance and Standard Oil wanted their own skyscrapers. In the late 1960s, Sears, Roebuck & Company joined that trend.

At the time, Sears was the world's largest company selling products to people. Its department stores and catalogs offered everything from socks to refrigerators. The company had a large group of buildings on Chicago's West Side. But the company wanted to move its headquarters into downtown Chicago. In 1968 Sears bought an entire city block on the western edge of downtown. Stores, warehouses, and even part of a street were torn down to clear the way for the tower.

A TALL ORDER

As the first step in planning its new headquarters, Sears hired an interior design company, Environetics. Environetics designers studied how Sears's office workers used their space every day. They learned how many workers each department had. They saw what equipment workers used. They watched how people traffic flowed through offices. They talked to Sears executives to learn how much the company planned to grow in the next ten or twenty years.

Environetics told Sears that the company would need about 4 million square feet (371,612 sq. m). Half would be for present workers and half for the future. Sears executives realized that much space would mean a very tall building. In 1969 Sears hired the Chicago architectural firm of Skidmore, Owings & Merrill (SOM) to plan the tower.

Older office buildings had many inside walls, columns, and doorways. These held up the horizontal beams that formed floors and ceilings. But modern companies wanted floor plans with large open spaces and fewer dividing walls and columns. Removing interior walls and columns left architects with a problem. What would hold up each story's ceiling?

SOM's chief engineer, Fazlur Khan, came up with one solution. Khan designed a system called bundled tubes. Skyscrapers could be built as a group of straight-sided upright tubes bound together by trusses (steel bands). The walls of one tube would back up to and support the walls of another tube. The tube walls would do the job of interior walls and columns.

In 1970 SOM engineers and architects had used bundled tubes to build the John Hancock Center. This one-hundred-story building sits on Chicago's North Michigan Avenue. The Hancock Center's bundled tube construction became the model for the Sears Tower.

THE DESIGN

Khan and SOM architect Bruce Graham decided that the Sears Tower would have nine tubes bundled together. Each tube would be a 75-foot (23 m) square. All the tubes would rise to a height of forty-nine stories. Three tubes would end at this height. The rest would end at higher floors. Only two would rise to the full height of ninety-five stories.

With this design, the floor space decreases as the tower rises. Sears could use the larger lower floors. The company could rent the smaller upper floors until it needed them. The outside open spaces created where tubes ended are called setbacks. The setbacks gave the tower a unique look.

When the steel tubes and trusses were finished, the building was covered in black aluminum and dark-tinted windows. This type of smooth exterior is called a curtain wall. Curtain walls add to a skyscraper's upright look.

A RECORD BREAKER

As SOM architects neared the end of their planning stage, they realized something. At ninety-five stories, the Sears Tower would only be about ten stories short of the World Trade Center (WTC). The two towers of the WTC were still being built in New York City. When they were finished, their height would be 1,368 feet (417 m). Then the twin towers would become the world's tallest buildings. SOM architects changed their plans and added another fifteen floors to the Sears Tower. When finished, it would stand at 1,450 feet (442 m). That was the highest the tower could go. If higher, it would interfere with Chicago airplane traffic.

Workers broke ground for the Sears Tower in August 1970. To build the foundation, they built a wall 3 feet (1 m) deep around the outside of the site. Inside the wall, they dug a hole 50 feet (15 m) deep. The workers then drilled 114 holes another 50 feet into the ground until they hit bedrock. The holes were lined with steel and filled with concrete. These holes anchored the foundation of the building. After the foundation was complete, workers began building the tubes and trusses.

For the exterior walls, trucks hauled in prefabricated steel pieces. Each piece was made of a 25-foot (7.5 m) vertical beam crossed by two 15-foot (4.5 m) horizontal beams. Workers called these Christmas trees. Each Christmas tree was welded to the next to form the tower's steel frame. Other workers constructed the floors by pouring concrete into forms built over the steel truss beams.

Soaring Skyward

Chicagoans watched in amazement as the tower rose eight stories each month. Creeper cranes lifted the Christmas trees and other construction materials. Workers welded and pounded pieces into place. As the tower neared completion, workers began adding fireproofing to the outside walls of the lower floors. Then they hung the tinted glass in sections. Before the upper floors were even enclosed, workers were installing cabinets and carpets on the lower floors.

In spring 1973, workers finished framing the top floor. On May 3, the last beam was ready to be lifted more than 1,400 feet (427 m) into the air. At a special ceremony, Chicago mayor Richard J. Daley and thousands of Sears employees signed the beam. Workers lifted the beam and bolted it into place.

Workers still had to add exterior walls to the top floors. They also had to finish the interior and landscape the area around the tower's base. But major construction on the Sears Tower was complete.

An Amazing View

Sears employees and renters began moving into the Sears Tower in fall 1973. They used the tower's 104 elevators to get to their offices. The enormous flow

An iron worker balances on a cable as construction continues on the top floors of the Sears Tower in 1973.

of workers in and out of the tower brought new life to that part of downtown. Soon new shops and restaurants opened nearby.

In 1974 the Sears Tower Skydeck opened to the public. The Skydeck is an observation deck on the tower's 103rd floor. On the Skydeck, visitors stand 1,353 feet (412 m) above the sidewalk. Floor-to-ceiling windows and telescopes show views of the city and the lake. Interactive exhibits detail Chicago's history, famous people, and landmarks.

In 1982 Sears added two antennas. The white antennas raised the overall height of the tower to 1,730 feet (527 m). Thirty radio and television stations use the antennas to transmit signals.

Sears, Roebuck did not stay downtown. Its business did not grow as much as expected, and it did not need all that space. In 1992 the company sold the tower and moved to the suburbs.

In the 2000s, more than one hundred companies rent offices in the Sears Tower. On average, more than ten thousand people work, do business, eat, and shop in the tower every day. In 2009 the tower's owners announced plans to make this busy center more energy-efficient. As a first step, wind turbines and solar panels will be installed on the building's setback roofs. Those systems will convert wind and solar power into electricity for the building. Over a five-year period, the tower's heating, cooling, and lighting systems will be updated. The owners hope to reduce the tower's need for outside electricity by 80 percent.

An exciting update to the Skydeck was also unveiled. About 1.3 million people every year take the zooming elevators to the Skydeck. Beginning in

In 2000 four more antennas were added to the corners of the Sears Tower roof. The new antennas are 29 feet (9 m) high and mounted on 80-foot (24 m) bases. They were added to accommodate signals for high-definition television (HDTV).

THE *Willis* TOWER?

In March 2009, British insurance company the Willis Group announced that it would be moving into the Sears Tower. More than five hundred Willis employees would occupy about three floors. Willis also announced that it had bought naming rights to the building. The Sears Tower would become the Willis Tower. The announcement was not popular among Chicagoans. Many saw it as a lack of respect for a city landmark.

A poll conducted by the Chicago Tribune suggested that 95 percent of people surveyed were against the renaming. And a campaign against the name change on the Facebook online network drew more than 95,000 members. The Willis Group expressed surprise at the negative reaction. But in July 2009, the building was renamed as planned. Whether Chicagoans will actually begin using "the Willis Tower" remains to be seen.

In 2009 the Sears Tower opened a new attraction: the Ledge. These glass cubes jut out from the Skydeck, giving visitors an amazing view of Chicago.

July 2009, visitors with strong stomachs can step out onto the Ledge. The Ledge is a set of four all-glass balconies on the Skydeck's west side. Through the Ledge's glass floors, visitors can look straight down 103 stories from the top of Chicago's architectural wonder.

5 THE SYDNEY *Opera House*

The Sydney Opera House in Australia is
a premier destination for music lovers and
performers alike. The building quickly became
a symbol of Sydney's vibrant culture.

Until the 1600s, the continent of Australia was unknown to most Europeans. It is on the other side of the world from Europe. Europeans could only guess at what lay "down under." But in the 1600s and 1700s, Dutch and English sailors began exploring Australia's coasts. In 1788 British ships sailed into a sheltered part of the southeastern coast. There they established the town of Sydney. For more than fifty years, Great Britain used Sydney as a place to send prisoners from overcrowded British jails.

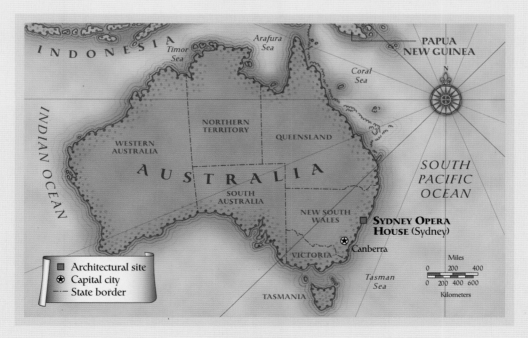

INDONESIA

Timor Sea

Arafura Sea

PAPUA NEW GUINEA

Coral Sea

N

INDIAN OCEAN

NORTHERN TERRITORY

QUEENSLAND

WESTERN AUSTRALIA

A U S T R A L I A

SOUTH PACIFIC OCEAN

SOUTH AUSTRALIA

NEW SOUTH WALES

SYDNEY OPERA HOUSE (Sydney)

VICTORIA

Canberra

TASMANIA

Tasman Sea

■ Architectural site
✪ Capital city
--- State border

Miles
0   200   400
0 200 400 600
Kilometers

Sydney has come a long way since its days as a prison town. Modern-day Sydney has more than four million residents. It is the capital of the Australian state of New South Wales (NSW). Sydney has become one of the most famous cities in the world, with parks, gardens, universities, and museums. It is also home to the beautiful Sydney Opera House.

ON THE WATERFRONT

The city of Sydney was built in a natural bay called Port Jackson. Port Jackson includes Sydney Harbor and Sydney Cove. On the southern edge of Sydney Cove is a jut of land called Bennelong Point. In the mid-1950s, Bennelong Point was chosen as the site of the city's new performing arts center, the Sydney Opera House.

Planning and construction of the opera house took almost twenty years. The director of the Sydney Symphony Orchestra, Eugene Goossens, first suggested the project. Goossens wanted a place that would draw all kinds of people to hear classical music. Other leaders in Sydney agreed. Joseph Cahill, the premier (political leader) of NSW, also wanted to bring an important architectural project to Sydney.

In January 1956, Cahill announced a contest. Architects from around the world were invited to submit plans for the new opera house. The contest announcement included a twenty-five-page book describing the

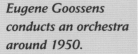

Eugene Goossens conducts an orchestra around 1950.

Jorn Utzon, designer of the Sydney Opera House, studied architecture at the Royal Danish Academy of Fine Arts in Copenhagen, Denmark.

ARCHITECTURAL *Expression*

The Sydney Opera House is often classified as a type of modern architecture called expressionist. Expressionist architecture often uses symbolic shapes. The shapes can be twisted, curved, lengthened, and shortened to express emotion. Expressionism is also found in art, movies, and music.

features the opera house should include. Four famous architects were brought in as judges. The judging committee received more than two hundred plans from architects in thirty-two countries.

In January 1957, the judges chose a Danish architect named Jorn Utzon as the winner. Utzon was surprised by the news. His drawings had been very simple. They did not follow all the rules described in the contest book. But the judges liked his unique concept. Utzon moved to Sydney to begin work on the project.

Utzon's design began with a raised platform called a podium. A group of buildings would sit on top of the podium. The podium would house all the workings of the performance center. This included dressing rooms, rehearsal rooms, and storage. One of the two largest buildings would contain a combined opera house and concert hall. The other would be a separate theater for plays.

The roofs of the buildings were designed as a series of very large shapes. These curved structures would be covered in white tiles to resemble the sails of a ship. The roofs would show Sydney's connection to the sea. An engineering firm, Ove Arup and Partners, was hired to translate Utzon's design into a building plan.

WORK BEGINS

Construction on the opera house began in the spring of 1959. Work crews laid the opera house foundation by sinking 588 concrete piles (columns) into the ground. The piles supported the podium. The opera house's two main buildings would sit on the podium facing the harbor. Smaller buildings would be built to the sides.

Soon after work began, Ove Arup engineers ran into problems. They were having serious trouble making a construction plan for the large curved shapes that Utzon designed. Utzon changed his design to use shapes that would be easier to build.

He used a sphere as the basic shape of his design. The roofs would all be segments—or arcs—of that sphere. The arcs would be supported by ribs that rose from a solid base. The roof segments and ribs would be prefabricated concrete. Glass curtain walls would hang from the roof shells, covering the fronts and filling in side spaces between the segments. Building on the main halls began in 1963.

INTERIOR SPACES

Utzon had grand plans for the interior of the opera house halls. Huge windows would overlook the harbor in common areas. Patrons

FRUIT *Peels*

The outside of the opera house symbolizes Sydney's connection to the sea. But for the actual geometry of the roof segments, Utzon was inspired while peeling an orange. The round shape of the orange can be broken into curved pieces of peel. Utzon wanted his roof segments to follow that same pattern.

The main walls of the Sydney Opera House begin to rise during construction in 1964.

would gather here before performances. Hallways and sweeping granite staircases would lead patrons into the performance areas. The interiors of the performance areas were to be decorated with strong colors that reflected Australia's natural beauty.

But appearances were only part of the plan. Acoustics (the science of how sound travels) is important in buildings used for music, singing, and acting. Utzon wanted the buildings' acoustics to be designed to fit with the architecture. He began work on a system of plywood wedges that followed the shape of the roof. Sound waves traveling from the stages would reflect off the plywood. The wedges would provide perfect acoustics.

TROUBLES

But before Utzon got far, the entire opera house project ran into trouble. Government elections were held in 1965, and a new government was elected. The opera house project came under the control of a new government official, Davis Hughes. Hughes believed that the project was wasting money. He did not like Utzon's designs. He also did not believe that the estimated schedules and budgets were correct. Hughes stopped paying Utzon. In 1966 Utzon was forced to resign.

Scaffolding covers the outer shells of the opera house during the tiling stage in 1966.

Utzon left Australia. Hughes appointed architect Peter Hall to take over the project. By January 1967, the outer shells were finished and tiled. But plans for the plywood ceilings were canceled. This left the problem of acoustics unsolved. Hall spent three months traveling to concert halls around the world to study the issue.

Hall's solution was to limit the type of performances held in the Major Hall and Minor Hall. The Major Hall would be used for concerts, and the Minor Hall would be used for opera. The theater would move into a smaller space inside the podium. Each hall could then be tailored for acoustics, audience size, and the amount of space needed for musicians.

Hall also changed Utzon's plans for interior design. The seats in all the performance spaces have brightly colored upholstery. But the opera hall's walls were painted black. Balcony boxes were formed from plain concrete. The foyer (common area in front) of the theater was closed in, without any natural light or views of the harbor.

The Opera Theatre seats 1,507 people. The space is best used for opera, ballet, and modern dance performances. Opera Australia and the Australian Ballet Company perform here.

The Concert Hall seats 2,679 people. It is the largest hall at the Sydney Opera House. The Sydney Symphony, the Australian Chamber Orchestra, and the Sydney Philharmonia Choirs perform here.

Putting Hall's new plans into action took four years. The changes also resulted in cost increases. It became much more expensive than Utzon's original plan.

GRAND OPENING

The Sydney Opera House opened in 1973. Queen Elizabeth II of Great Britain led the ceremony. Jorn Utzon was awarded a gold medal by the Royal Institute of Architects Australia. But he refused to attend the opening.

Despite construction troubles, the opera house became a source of pride for Sydney residents. As Eugene Goossens planned, the opera house drew many Australians to performances. These included ones by Opera Australia, the Australian Ballet Company, the Sydney Dance Company, and the Sydney Theatre Company. The opera house also became a popular place for movie screenings, comedy performances, and rock and pop concerts. Each New Year's Eve, Sydney residents gather at the opera house's outdoor spaces for music and fireworks.

"It is impossible to think of Sydney without, at the same time, bringing to mind its opera house."
—Philip Drew, Australian architecture historian, 1995

UTZON'S VISION RETURNS

In 1999 the government of NSW and the Sydney Opera House Trust (the organization that runs the opera house) approached Utzon. They asked Utzon to develop a set of design principles. The design principles would serve as guidelines for all future changes to the buildings. They would ensure that changes are made in keeping with Utzon's vision.

Utzon replied that he was very pleased to be asked. But at eighty-one, he felt that he was unable to travel all the way from Denmark to Australia. Instead, his two sons, Jan and Klim (also architects), and his daughter Lin (an artist) would relay his plans and ideas to the trust.

In March 2003, the University of Sydney awarded Utzon an honorary degree for his work on the opera house. Later that year, he received the Pritzker Architecture Prize—the highest honor in the field of architecture—for his opera house design. In 2004 the Reception Hall at the opera house was renamed the Utzon Room.

In 2006 one of Utzon's redesign projects was finished. The project involved the theater's dark, crowded foyer. Workers cut six large windows and

Huge windows draw light into the interior of the opera house.

Fireworks explode over Sydney Harbor during New Year's celebrations in 2001.

three glass doors in the thick walls of the podium. On the outside, the area was framed with a row of columns. Theatergoers could enjoy natural light and open views of the harbor.

Utzon also began work on plans to improve the opera hall's seating and acoustics. The plan involves lowering the floor to make more room for musicians and seating. A future project will make the entire complex more accessible for visitors with limited movement (such as people in wheelchairs).

Utzon never returned to Australia after he resigned from the Sydney Opera House project. He has never set foot in the building that made him a world-famous architect. But Jan Utzon has said that his father "lives and breathes the opera house, and as its creator, he just has to close his eyes to see it."

"The sun did not know how beautiful its light was until it was reflected off this building."
—*Louis I. Kahn, architect, 1973*

6 Burj al Arab

The Burj al Arab Hotel in Dubai blends ancient symbols and modern materials in its soaring design.

$\mathcal{D}$UBAI IS A CITY IN THE UNITED ARAB EMIRATES. DUBAI SITS ON THE SOUTHEASTERN SHORE OF THE PERSIAN GULF. FOR CENTURIES DUBAI HAS RELIED ON THE SEA. DUBAI WAS ONCE A FISHING VILLAGE AND THEN A SMALL TRADING PORT. ALONG DUBAI'S COAST, THE BLUE GREEN GULF WATER WAS DOTTED WITH THE WHITE SAILS OF DHOWS, TRADITIONAL ARABIAN SHIPS.

In the late twentieth century, the city grew. It expanded away from the shore. But the people of Dubai wanted to stay close to the water. The city began building artificial islands along the coast. On one of those islands stands an amazing hotel. The Burj al Arab Hotel combines the old and the new. It was built using very modern materials and techniques. But it is designed to look like the billowing sail of a dhow, calling to mind Dubai's ancient connection to the sea.

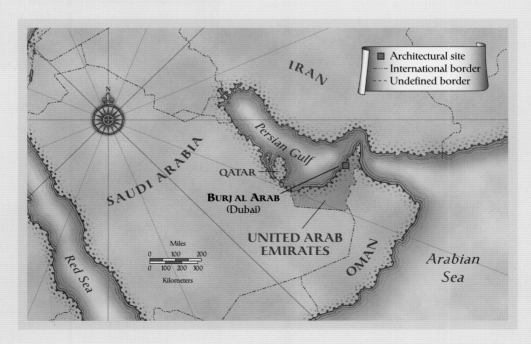

A SYMBOL FOR DUBAI

In the 1960s, oil and natural gas were discovered beneath the Arabian Peninsula. The discovery made the region's states and kingdoms very wealthy. In 1971 seven of those small, independent states banded together to form the UAE. The UAE is one of the richest countries in the world.

Dubai is one of the states. It is also the name of that state's largest city. But Dubai is not completely dependent on oil and gas. It has a long tradition as a center of international trade. In the 1900s and early 2000s, that trade brought many foreign visitors and workers to Dubai.

International trade and contact with foreign peoples has shaped Dubai's culture. Its leaders encourage economic growth in areas such as real estate and tourism. It sees itself as a center for upscale tourism. This kind of tourism features expensive shopping centers, entertainment events, and luxurious beach resorts.

DID YOU *Know?*

More than 80 percent of the people living in the city of Dubai are foreigners. They come from almost two hundred countries. These include India, Iran, Kuwait, the Philippines, and Great Britain. The UAE does not allow any foreigners to become citizens. And foreigners can only rent—not own—shops, offices, and homes. But the UAE prides itself on having a welcoming culture. English and Hindi (an Indian language) are widely spoken. And international sports, music, and food are very popular.

The Dubai skyline rises above the harbor at sunrise. Some of the city's most impressive buildings overlook the waterfront.

In the early 1990s, Dubai's leader, Sheikh Muhammed bin Rashid al Maktoum, wanted Dubai to have a building of outstanding architectural design. The sheikh hired the British architectural firm W. S. Atkins. Atkins architect Tom Wright understood what the sheikh was looking for. The project should be symbolic of Dubai, the way the Eiffel Tower is a symbol of Paris, France, or the Opera House is a symbol of Sydney, Australia.

Wright was sitting at a beach café in Dubai in 1993. He sketched out a tall, sail-shaped building on a paper napkin. From there, he developed a more detailed drawing. Then he made a paper model of the building. He showed these to the sheikh and other leaders in October 1993. The design was a success. Dubai's leaders hired a South African company, Murray & Roberts, to oversee construction.

BUILDING THE ISLAND

Officials named the proposed hotel Burj al Arab—Arabic for "the Arabian Tower." It was to be part of the Jumeirah beach area. But Wright did not want to build the hotel right on the beach. It would block out the beach's sun for most of the day. Instead, they would build the hotel on an artificial island 919 feet (280 m) offshore. A winding causeway (road raised above the water) would connect the beach and the island.

"We decided that the test to determine if a building is symbolic is if you can draw it in five seconds and everyone recognizes it."

—Tom Wright, on the theory behind his unique design for Burj al Arab, 1994

Workers began building the island in 1994. They first sank temporary piles into the seabed. They then put banks of large rocks around the piles. This formed a sort of pool. For the next step, the seawater was removed from the center of the pool. It was replaced by a layer of rocks. Workers laid concrete webbing around the outer edge of the banks. The webbing keeps the foundation rocks from washing away. It also breaks the waves as they hit the island.

Construction workers drove 250 permanent piles 131 feet (40 m) through this rock foundation and into the seabed. They then laid a concrete floor 6.5 feet (2 m) thick at the base of the island. They added walls around the piles to keep out sand and rock. The floor and walls formed the basement of the hotel. Construction of the island took three years.

BUILDING THE HOTEL

After the island was built, workers began constructing the hotel. To make the building look like a billowing sail, Wright designed it as a triangle. In the right-angle corner of the triangle is the sail's "mast." It is a 1,050-foot (321 m) steel post. Curving out from the mast are two steel supports. The mast and supports form the tower's skeleton.

The hotel's 202 duplex (two-story) guest rooms line two sides of the triangle. The outer walls of these sides are enclosed in tinted glass. This gives hotel guests wide views of the Persian Gulf.

The third wall of the triangle faces the beach. The center of the triangle is an open area called an atrium. In many buildings, atriums are only two or three stories high. Burj al Arab's atrium runs all the way to the top floor. At 597 feet (182 m), it is the tallest atrium in the world.

Massive steel supports create Burj al Arab's distinctive sail shape.

The third wall has no rooms. Its towering stretch of empty wall emphasizes the height of the atrium. It also represents the billowing curve of the sail.

The third wall gave Wright a design challenge and a chance to create a completely unique feature. If Wright used glass to cover the wall, the sun would beat down on the atrium all day. If he used concrete, it would take away from the effect of a curving sail. Wright's solution was to cover the third wall with two layers of white fiberglass cloth coated in Teflon. Fiberglass is a flexible fabric strengthened by tiny bits of glass. Teflon is a plasticlike coating. The fabric lets in light while keeping out glare. The Teflon prevents dirt and sand from sticking to the wall.

The fiberglass wall is supported by truss beams that form two huge Xs, one stacked on top of the other. The supports were built off-site and carried to the island on special trucks. It took workers one whole day to lift the second X into place.

THE LAP OF LUXURY

Construction was completed in 1999. Khuan Chew of KCA International was hired as the interior designer. Chew used traditional Arab design elements inside. They included pointed arches and star shapes. But she also used many elements from other cultures, such as Italian marble and crystal chandeliers.

The Burj al Arab was built to be one of the most expensive hotels in the world. The guest suites (sets of rooms) are large and luxurious. Most have full dining and living rooms. Some have cocktail bars, libraries, private movie theaters, and pool tables. Guests can arrange in-room meals with a personal chef. At night a special hotel employee arrives with a pillow menu. Guests can pick from thirteen different kinds of pillows.

GETTING *There*

The causeway to Burj al Arab's island is private. You're not allowed on the causeway if you're not a registered guest or don't have reservations at one of the hotels' restaurants. If you are a guest, the hotel makes sure you arrive in style. Visitors are picked up at the airport in a chauffeured Rolls Royce (a very expensive car). Or they can be flown in a helicopter directly to the hotel's private helipad (landing area). The helipad extends out from the hotel 689 feet (210 m) above the ground.

The hotel's helipad has become famous on its own in recent years. In 2005 the helipad was temporarily converted to a grass court for tennis stars Andre Agassi and Roger Federer (below).

Visitors to the Al Mahara restaurant at Burj al Arab can dine next to a huge aquarium. "Al Mahara" means "the oyster" in Arabic.

The Burj al Arab's restaurants are also unique. The Skybar extends like a metal tube from the hotel's twenty-seventh floor. At 650 feet (200 m) above sea level, the bar has amazing views of the gulf. The Al Mahara restaurant offers guests another amazing view of the sea. In the center of the restaurant sits a 35,000-cubic-foot (990 cu. m) seawater aquarium. It has curved Plexiglas walls.

MEGATALLS

Dubai continues to bring architectural fame to the UAE. Many recent plans have focused on megatall, or super-tall, buildings. The Burj Dubai is due to be finished in 2010. The top of its tower will be 2,684 feet (818 m) high. Dubai's Princess Tower (1,358 feet, or 414 m) will follow in 2011. Other megatall projects scheduled for Dubai's future include Marina 101, 23 Marina, the Emirates Park towers, and the Elite Residence.

These tall spires will all pass the Burj al Arab in height. But the Burj al Arab achieves what its architect set out to do. They created an instantly recognizable building for Dubai. The Burj al Arab will remain a symbol of the city and an architectural wonder.

7 Taipei 101

Taipei 101 glows above the Taipei skyline at night.

$\mathcal{T}$AIWAN ISLAND LIES IN THE PACIFIC OCEAN, OFF THE COAST OF MAINLAND CHINA. THE ISLAND HAS TOWERING MOUNTAIN CLIFFS, FARMLAND, AND TROPICAL FORESTS. IT ALSO HAS EXTREME WEATHER AND FREQUENT EARTHQUAKES. ABOUT TWENTY EARTHQUAKES HIT TAIWAN EACH MONTH. THIS DOES NOT MAKE THE ISLAND AN IDEAL SPOT FOR ONE OF THE WORLD'S TALLEST SKYSCRAPERS. YET IN THE CAPITAL CITY OF TAIPEI, TAIPEI 101 RISES 1,667 FEET (508 M)—AN ENGINEERING AND ARCHITECTURAL WONDER.

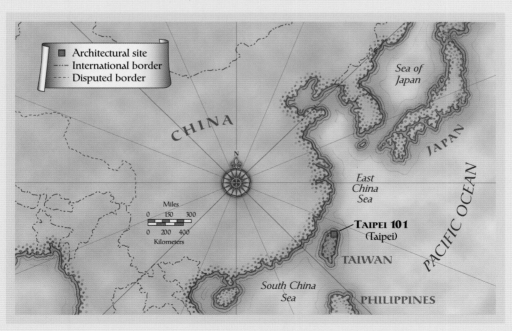

TAIWAN

Taiwan and mainland China share a close history. In fact, Taiwan's official name is the Republic of China (ROC). The ROC governs Taiwan Island and several smaller groups of nearby islands. The ROC once also governed mainland China. But after World War II, China was divided by a civil war. The Kuomintang (KMT), a political party, fought against the Communist Party. In 1949 Communist forces took control of mainland China. The KMT fled to Taiwan.

Mainland China became known as the People's Republic of China (PRC). Taiwan became the ROC. The KMT made Taipei its capital. The PRC still considers Taiwan part of China. It only recognizes Taiwan's government as a local government.

Despite these political tensions, Taiwan and China are culturally close. Most of Taiwan's 23 million people are ethnic Han Chinese, the main ethnic group of China. Taiwan's official language is Mandarin, a Chinese dialect. Most people also speak Taiwanese, another Chinese dialect. And many Taiwanese people practice the Chinese religions of Buddhism, Confucianism, and Taoism.

But unlike China, Taiwan has long-standing relations with much of the rest of the world. It has a democratically elected government. Its economy relies on exports and international trade. Exports and industry made Taiwan's economy very strong. In the 1990s and early 2000s, services have also become an important part of the economy. About 60 percent of Taiwan's economy is based on services, such as banks, finance companies, and insurance companies.

TAIPEI

Taiwan's strong economy has improved the lives of many Taiwanese. Personal income, education levels, and health care have all steadily improved since the 1950s. The island's increasing prosperity has allowed cities such as Taipei to grow as financial and cultural centers.

Taipei is located at the northern tip of the island. It is Taiwan's largest city, with 2.6 million residents. The city is home to National Taiwan University, the Presidential Building, the National Central Library, the Taipei World Trade Center, and other important government, business, and cultural buildings.

In 1997 the Taipei city government began plans for Taipei 101. It was planned for 101 floors. The city was developing a new business area, the Hsinyi District. Taipei's mayor, Chen Shui-bian, wanted a tower as a landmark and a business center for Hsinyi. In October the city government signed a contract with C. Y. Lee & Partners, a Taiwanese architectural firm.

Designing a 101-floor tower was a challenge. Every year, Taiwan is subject to monsoons (winds that bring heavy rain and winter cold) and typhoons (hurricanes). The storms can produce winds up to 100 miles (161 kilometers) per hour. In addition, the construction site was only 650 feet (200 m) from an

The Taipei 101 tower stands in the background of this portrait of C. Y. Lee of C. Y. Lee & Partners. Lee also designed the Tuntex Sky Tower, which was Taiwan's tallest building until the completion of Taipei 101.

earthquake fault (a crack or weakness in Earth's crust). Taipei 101 would have to be flexible enough to withstand high winds. It would also have to be strong enough to survive earthquakes.

Typhoon Krosa hit Taipei in 2007. The storm killed four people and damaged homes and businesses throughout the city.

A MEGASTRUCTURE

Building so close to a fault line seemed risky. But geologists knew that bedrock lay 197 feet (60 m) underground. The bedrock would provide a stable foundation. Lee engineers and architects planned to use new building technology to help steady the tower.

In January 1998, builders broke ground at the construction site. Workers drove 380 concrete piles 260 feet (80 m) into the ground. This was deep enough to anchor the building in the bedrock. On top of that foundation, workers began building a steel megaframe.

The megaframe consisted of sixteen steel columns that form a core at the center of the tower. Near the outside walls, workers built eight super columns. The inner columns were filled with concrete up to the sixty-second floor to increase their strength. The outer super columns were filled with concrete to the twenty-sixth floor. Every eight floors, the inner and outer columns are connected by beams called outrigger trusses. The trusses steady the tower without making it rigid.

In March 2002, during construction, an earthquake hit Taiwan. The quake knocked two construction cranes off the tower. Five workers were killed. The loss of life was tragic. But there was no damage to the building. This seemed to be proof that the tower's design would do what it was meant to do.

AN ASIAN TOWER

For the exterior design, the architects combined Asian culture with modern international architecture. The tower is divided into eight sections stacked one above the other. In Chinese culture, the number eight is a sign of prosperity. The eight sections each bow outward slightly at the top. The architects felt that this design called to mind a pagoda. This is a kind of traditional tower found throughout Asia. The design also resembles a bamboo stalk. In Asia, bamboo is a symbol of strength.

Builders covered the exterior with a glass curtain wall. The green glass provides protection from UV (ultraviolet) sunlight. It also helps keep the building cool. Green is the color of jade, a stone used in Asian art and jewelry.

To finish the curtain wall, four silver design elements were added to each section. The silver shapes are called *ruyi*. In Chinese culture, ruyi are meant to look like heavenly clouds. They stand for contentment and protection.

Feng Shui

Some Asian cultures observe an ancient practice called feng shui. According to feng shui, human efforts should work with an environment's natural energy. It is believed that following feng shui rules will bring good luck, health, and prosperity.

After architects finished their plans for Taipei 101, feng shui experts were hired to go over the project. According to the plans, the tower faced south—a good direction. But the experts were concerned that a road ran right into the construction site. That could bring bad luck or illness to the building's occupants. Designers fixed the problem by installing a fountain in front of the door. The fountain blocks the road and directs good energy into the tower.

Silver ruyi stand out against the green glass curtain walls of Taipei 101.

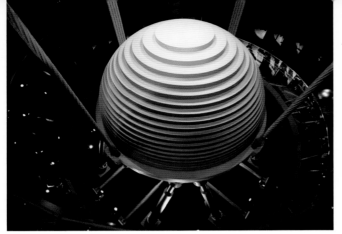

When construction was done, builders added what many consider the building's most amazing feature. They hung an enormous gold-colored steel ball from steel cables between the eighty-seventh and ninety-first floors. The steel ball is called a tuned mass damper (TMD). Taipei 101's TMD is 18 feet (5.5 m) in diameter. It weighs 730 tons (660 metric tons). The TMD is designed to reduce building sway by up to 40 percent. When the building sways in high winds, the TMD swings in the opposite direction. This helps to balance the building's movement. It is the world's largest and heaviest TMD.

A BIG DRAW

Taipei 101 officially opened on December 31, 2004. The tower is a multiuse building. It houses offices, stores, shops, and restaurants. Most of the building's floors—nine through eighty-four—are offices rented by various companies. About ten thousand workers occupy the building every workday. But the tower is also a big draw to visitors and tourists.

Sixty-three elevators serve the tower's human traffic. Two elevators take visitors from the fifth floor to the observation decks on the eighty-ninth and ninety-first floors. These are the fastest elevators in the world, traveling at 3,314 feet (1,010 m) per minute. The ride lasts only thirty-seven seconds.

The ninety-first floor observatory is outdoors. Visitors can see the city, nearby mountains, the Keelung River, and the South China Sea. They also have an up-close view of the tower's 60-foot (18 m) spire. The eighty-ninth floor observatory is indoors. On this floor, audio guides in eight languages and high-powered binoculars add to the view. This floor also has gift shops and special mailboxes where tourists can send "greetings from the sky." On the eighty-eighth floor, visitors can walk all the way around the TMD.

But not all the tower's attractions are at the top. Six floors at the bottom of Taipei 101 are occupied by the 101 Mall. This shopping mall has more than 160 stores and twelve restaurants. The stores range from shops you might see in any U.S. mall to some of the world's most expensive clothing and jewelry boutiques. The mall is very popular with young Taipei residents as well as with tourists.

In 2008 Burj Dubai tower in the UAE passed Taipei 101 in height. But that same year, Taipei 101 was named by *Newsweek* magazine as one the New Seven Wonders of the World. The tower remains the pride of Taiwan and an architectural and engineering marvel.

On New Year's Eve in 2008, more than ten thousand fireworks were launched from Taipei 101. The tower is at the center of the city's New Year's celebrations.

TIMELINE

326   Emperor Constantine orders construction of a church over Saint Peter's grave.

1400s   The Renaissance develops in Italy and begins to spread through Europe.

1505   Pope Julius II hires Donato Bramante to build a new, grander Saint Peter's.

1547   Michelangelo Buonarroti takes over Saint Peter's construction and designs its concrete dome.

1648   The Taj Mahal in Agra, India, is completed.

1667   Gianlorenzo Bernini finishes Saint Peter's Square.

1750s   The Industrial Revolution begins in Great Britain.

1788   Great Britain establishes Sydney, Australia, as a prison colony.

1857   The first passenger elevator is installed in a New York City department store.

1880   German engineer Werner von Siemens develops an electric elevator system.

1885   In Chicago, Illinois, U.S. architect William Le Baron Jenney uses steel framing to construct the city's first skyscraper.

1889   The Eiffel Tower in Paris, France, is completed.

1949   Taiwan becomes the seat of the Republic of China (ROC).

1971   The United Arab Emirates (UAE), a federation of seven states, forms as an independent country.

1973   The Sears Tower in Chicago opens. The Sydney Opera House opens in Sydney, Australia.

1982   UNESCO lists the Taj Mahal as a World Heritage Site.

1999   The Burj al Arab in Dubai, UAE, opens.

2004   Taipei 101 in Taipei, Taiwan, opens.

2007   Taipei 101 is named by *Newsweek* magazine as one the New Seven Wonders of the World. UNESCO lists the Sydney Opera House as a World Heritage Site.

2009   Burj Dubai tower in the UAE reaches 2,625 feet (800 m).

        The Sears Tower is renamed the Willis Tower.

CHOOSE AN EIGHTH WONDER

Now that you've read about the seven architectural wonders of the modern world, do a little research to choose an eighth wonder. You may enjoy working with a friend.

To do your research, look at some of the websites and books listed on pages 76 and 77. Use the Internet and library books to look for more information on some of the other buildings mentioned in the book. What other buildings were designed by the architects mentioned in the book? And what are some other cities around the world that might have amazing architecture? Look for buildings that
- *are exceptionally beautiful*
- *used new building techniques or designs*
- *are unlike any other*
  building on Earth

You might even try gathering photos and writing your own chapter on the eighth wonder!

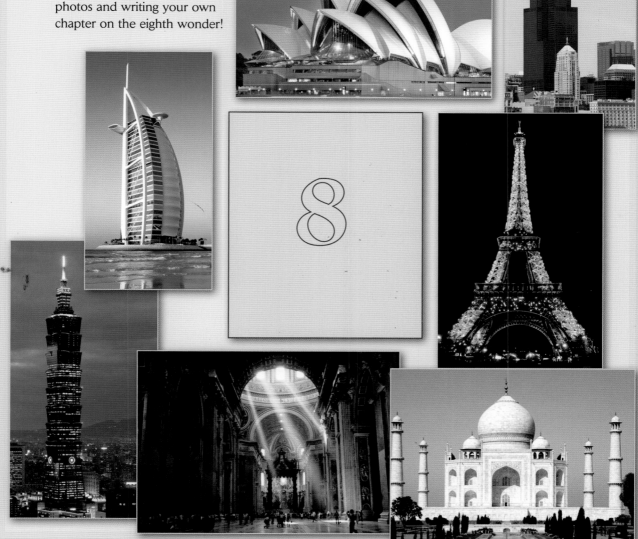

GLOSSARY

arch: a structure with two sides connected by a curved top

architect: someone who designs buildings

architecture: the design and the study of the design of buildings

atrium: an open area in the center of a building

basilica: an ancient Roman public hall or a Christian church used for special ceremonies

concrete: a stonelike building material that can be poured when wet and that dries strong and hard

construction: the building of structures

cranes: machines that pick up and move heavy materials

curtain wall: smooth exterior walls usually made of glass, metal, or stone facing. Curtain walls do not bear any of the weight of the building.

dome: a rounded roof or ceiling

engineer: someone who designs structures or systems, such as bridges or machines

expressionism: a modern style of architecture that uses symbolic shapes

Industrial Revolution: a movement to introduce newly invented machinery into factories. The Industrial Revolution began in Great Britain in the 1750s.

modernism: an architectural (and art) style that emphasizes simple shapes and decoration

piers: upright structures used to support a building

piles: columns used to build the foundations of buildings

prefabricated: made ahead of time. Prefabricated building pieces are later assembled on the construction site.

Renaissance: a historical period in Europe from the early 1400s to the early 1600s

steel: iron combined with elements such as carbon to make it harder, stronger, and easier to shape

technology: turning science into tools and inventions

truss: a beam or other structure that supports or strengthens

United Nations Educational, Scientific and Cultural Organization (UNESCO): an organization that helps protect sites that are important to the cultural heritage of all nations

vaulted ceiling: a ceiling or roof formed by a series of connected arches

welded: fastened into place using heated metal

world's fair: a large exhibition meant to showcase scientific discoveries, inventions, and cultural achievements. The first world fair was held in London, England, in 1851.

wrought iron: a very strong and rigid metal

SOURCE NOTES

15 Helen F. North, quoted in Robert Kahn, ed., *City Secrets: Rome* (New York: Little Bookroom, 1999).

20 Ebba Koch. *The Complete Taj Mahal and the Riverfront Gardens of Agra* (London: Thames & Hudson, 2006), 84.

23 William Sleeman, *Rambles and Recollections of an Indian Official* (rev. ed., London: Oxford University Press, 1915). Available at http://infomotions.com/etexts/gutenberg/dirs/1/5/4/8/15483/15483.htm.

30 Joseph Harriss. *The Tallest Tower: Eiffel and the Belle Epoque* (Boston: Houghton Mifflin, 1975), p. 21. Available at http://www.eiffel-tower.com/teiffel/uk/documentation/pdf/about_the%20Eiffel_Tower.pdf.

33 Ibid., 8.

33 Ibid.

33 Ibid., 22.

33 Ibid.

41 Gordon Metcalf, quoted in Rovert Enstad, "Girder Tops Sears 'Rock,'" *Chicago Tribune*, May 4, 1973, available online at http://www.searstower.org/articles.html#topped (July 10, 2009).

53 Philip Drew, *Sydney Opera House* (London: Phaidon Press, 1995), 4.

54 UNESCO, "World Heritage: The Sydney Opera House." UNESCO.org, n.d., http://whc.unesco.org/en/list/166 (July 21, 2009).

55 Jan Utzon, quoted in Sydney Opera House official website, n.d., http://www.sydneyoperahouse.com/about/the_architect.aspx (July 10, 2009).

55 Louis I. Kahn, quoted in Geraldine Brooks, "Unfinished Business," *New Yorker*, October 17, 2005. Available online at http://www.newyorker.com/archive/2005/10/17/051017fa_fact2 (July 10, 2009).

59 Tom Wright, "FAQ," tomwrightdesign.com, n.d., http://www.tomwrightdesign.com/web/burj_faq.php (October 19, 2008).

71 Dennis Poon, *All Things Considered,* interview by Melissa Block, December 30, 2004, NPR, 2009, available at http://www.npr.org/templates/story/story.php?storyId=4252073 (July 10, 2009).

SELECTED BIBLIOGRAPHY

Brooks, Geraldine. "Unfinished Business." *New Yorker*, October 17, 2005. Available online at http://www.newyorker.com/archive/2005/10/17/051017fa_fact2 (October 18, 2008).

Drew, Philip. *Sydney Opera House*. London: Phaidon Press, 1995.

Harriss, Joseph. *The Tallest Tower: Eiffel and the Belle Epoque*. Boston: Houghton Mifflin, 1975.

Koch, Ebba. *The Complete Taj Mahal and the Riverfront Gardens of Agra*. London: Thames & Hudson, 2006.

Lepik, Andres. *Skyscrapers*. Translated by Christine Shuttleworth. Munich: Prestel, 2004.

McPhee, Sarah. *Bernini and the Bell Towers*. New Haven, CT: Yale University Press, 2002.

Moynihan, Elizabeth B., ed. *The Moonlight Gardens: New Discoveries at the Taj Mahal*. Washington, DC: Smithsonian Institution, 2000.

Pridmore, Jay. *Sears Tower*. Rohnert Park, CA: Pomegranate Communications, 2002.

Scotti, R. A. *Basilica: The Splendor and the Scandal*. New York: Penguin, 2006.

Sydney Opera House. N.d. http://www.sydneyoperahouse.com/homepage.aspx (July 10, 2009).

Tom Wright Design. N.d. http://www.tomwrightdesign.com/index.php (July 10, 2009).

Watkin, David. *A History of Western Architecture*. 2nd ed. New York: Barnes and Noble Books, 1996.

FURTHER READING AND WEBSITES

Books

DuTemple, Lesley A. *The Taj Mahal*. Minneapolis: Twenty-First Century Books, 2003. Part of the Great Building Feats series, this book provides an in-depth look at the Shah Jahan, Mumtaz Mahal, and the building of the Taj Mahal.

Kent, Peter. *Great Building Stories of the Past*. Oxford: Oxford University Press, 2001. Kent explains the engineering and architecture behind some of history's great structures, including the Great Pyramid at Giza in Egypt, Beauvais Cathedral in France, the Brooklyn Bridge in New York, the Eiffel Tower in Paris, and Chek Lap Kok Airport in Hong Kong.

Visual Geography series. Minneapolis: Twenty-First Century Books, 2003–2010. Each book in this series details the geography, history, culture, and economy of a different country, including Australia, France, India, Taiwan, and the United States.

Wilkinson, Philip. *Building*. London: Dorling Kindersley, 2000. Part of the Eyewitness series, this book contains information on the details and element of world architecture from ancient to modern times.

Websites

Great Buildings Collection

http://www.greatbuildings.com/gbc.html

Architecture Week's Great Buildings Collection offers basic information on design style, materials, dates, and architects for buildings all over the world. Information is organized by buildings, architects, and places.

The Official Site of the Eiffel Tower

http://www.eiffel-tower.com/

This site contains practical information, a virtual 360-degree view of Paris, and a visitor's guide. The All You Need to Know about the Eiffel Tower section includes historical information, technical information, a complete reprint of the *Le Temps* letter of protest, and a timeline of famous visitors.

St. Peter's Basilica

http://www.stpetersbasilica.org/

This site provides detailed views of the basilica's art and architecture, floor plans and maps, and visitor's information.

Sydney Opera House

http://www.sydneyoperahouse.com/homepage.aspx

The official website of the Sydney Opera House offers detailed descriptions of the performance spaces, a gallery of photographs, information about Jorn Utzon, and a list of upcoming performances.

Taipei 101

http://www.taipei-101.com.tw/index_en.htm

The English-language version of Taipei 101's official site leads readers to diagrams of the tower, information about the tower's internal systems and tuned mass damper, and details of the tower's observatories and shopping mall.

INDEX

acoustics, 51
Agra, India, 19, 24
Al Mahara restaurant, 63
architects: Atkins, W. S., 59;
    Bartholdi, Auguste, 31;
    Bernini, Gianlorenzo, 14;
    Bramante, Donato, 10–12;
    della Porta, Giacomo,
    13; Eiffel, Gustave, 29;
    Graham, Bruce, 41; Hall,
    Peter, 52; Jenney, William
    Le Baron, 39; Khan,
    Fazlur, 41; Lee, C. Y., 67;
    Michaelangelo (Buonarroti),
    13; Murray & Roberts, 59;
    Ove Arup and Partners,
    49; Sanzio, Raphael, 13;
    Skidmore, Owings &
    Merrill, 40–41; Sullivan,
    Louis, 39; Utzon, Jorn,
    49–55; Wright, Tom, 59
architecture, 4–5
Atkins, W. S., 59
Australia, 47

Bartholdi, Auguste, 31
Basilica of Maxentius, 10, 11
Bernini, Gianlorenzo, 14
Black Taj, 24
Bramante, Donato, 10–12
bricks and mortar, 22
building materials: bricks and
    mortar, 22; bundled tubes,
    41; cement, 31; concrete,
    11; fiberglass cloth, 61;
    marble, 22; steel, 38;
    Teflon, 61; wrought iron,
    29
bundled tubes, 41
Burj al Arab Hotel, 56;
    construction, 59–61;
    location, 57; luxury
    features, 62–63; plans, 59
Burj Dubai tower, 71

Cahill, Joseph, 48
cement, 31
Chicago, Illinois, 37, 39
Chicago School, 39
China, 66–68

Christianity, 8, 11
church design, 11
Clement V (pope), 9
concrete, 11
Constantine, 8
cranes, 31, 43
cross, 10
curtain walls, 42
C. Y. Lee & Partners, 67

della Porta, Giacomo, 13
de Maupassant, Guy, 33
Dubai, United Arab Emirates,
    57, 58, 63

earthquakes, 68
Eiffel, Gustave, 29
Eiffel Tower, 26; construction,
    30–32; location, 27;
    maintenance, 34; modern
    uses, 35; plans, 29–30;
    protests, 33
elevators, 38
Elite Residence, 63
Emirates Park towers, 63
Environetics, 40
expressionist architecture, 49

feng shui, 69
fiberglass cloth, 61
France, 28

Goossens, Eugene, 48
Graham, Bruce, 41
Gregory XI (pope), 9

Hall, Peter, 52
helipads, 62

India, 17, 18
Industrial Revolution, 28
inlay, 23
islands, artificial, 59–60

Jenney, William Le Baron, 39
Jesus Christ, 8
Julius II (pope), 9–10, 12

Khan, Fazlur, 41
Khurram, 18–20

Lee, C. Y., 67

Maktoum, Muhammed bin
    Rashid al (sheikh), 59
marble, 22
Marina 101, 63
Masonic Temple, 39
megatall buildings, 63
Michaelangelo (Buonarroti),
    13
mihman khana, 22
minarets, 22
modernism, 38
Moderno, Carlo, 13–14
Mughal Empire, 18
Mumtaz Mahal, 18–19, 22,
    23
Murray & Roberts, 59

Nero, 8

Ove Arup and Partners, 49

Pantheon, 10
Paris, France, 27
Peter, Saint, 8
Piazza San Pietro, 15
Princess Tower, 63

radio, 35
Reliance Building, 39
Renaissance, 10
Republic of China (Taiwan),
    65, 66–68
Roman Catholic Church, 7,
    8–9
Rome, Italy, 7, 8, 15
Run Up (race), 70
ruyi, 69

Saint Peter's Basilica: building
    begins, 11–12; dome, 13–14;
    funding, 12; interior, 14;
    location, 7; piazza, 14–15;
    plans, 9–10; site, 8
Sanzio, Raphael, 13
Sears, Roebuck & Company,
    39–40
Sears Tower, 36; construction,
    43; facts, 45; location, 37;

occupancy, 43–44; plans, 40–42
Shah Jahan, 18–20, 24
Siemens, Werner von, 38
Sistine Chapel, 13
Skidmore, Owings & Merrill, 40–41
skyscrapers, modern, 38
Statue of Liberty, 31
steel, 38
Sullivan, Louis, 39
Sydney, Australia, 47
Sydney Opera House, 46; construction, 50–53; design, 48–49; interior, 50–51; location, 47; opening, 53
symmetry, 19

Tacoma Building, 39

Taipei, Taiwan, 66–68
Taipei 101, 64; construction, 68–70; features, 70–71; location, 65; plans, 67–68; tuned mass damper, 70
Taiwan Island, 65, 66–68
Taj Mahal, 5, 16; complex design, 21; construction begins, 19–20; exterior, 24; interior decorations, 23–24; legend of, 17; location, 17; mausoleum, 21–22; preservation, 25
Taj mosque, 22
Teflon, 61
Tiber River, 6
trusses, outrigger, 68
tuned mass damper, 70
Tuntex Sky Tower, 67
23 Marina, 63

United Arab Emirates (UAE), 57, 58
United Nations Educational, Scientific and Cultural Organization (UNESCO), 25
Utzon, Jorn, 49–55

Vatican City, 7, 12
vaulted ceilings, 11

websites, 76–77
World Heritage sites, 25
World's Fair (1889), 33–35
Wright, Tom, 59
wrought iron, 29
W. S. Atkins, 59

ABOUT THE AUTHOR

Ann Kerns has edited many nonfiction books for young readers and is the author of *Australia in Pictures, Romania in Pictures, Martha Stewart,* and *Troy.* She enjoys reading, travel, cooking, and music. A native of Illinois, she now lives in Minneapolis, Minnesota.

PHOTO ACKNOWLEDGMENTS

The images in this book are used with the permission of: © Dario Diament/Dreamstime.com, p. 5; © Murat Taner/Photographer's Choice/Getty Images, p. 6; © Laura Westlund/Independent Picture Service, pp. 7, 17, 27, 37, 47, 57, 65; St. Peter's, Vatican, Rome, Italy/The Bridgeman Art Library, p. 8; Scala/Art Resource, NY, p. 9; © Hulton Archive/Getty Images, p. 10 (top); © SuperStock/SuperStock, p. 10 (bottom); © Allan Friedlander/SuperStock, p. 11; Bildarchiv Preussischer Kulturbesitz/Art Resource, NY, p. 12; © Dario Mitidieri/The Image Bank/Getty Images, p. 14; © Miroslav Hasch/Dreamstime.com, p. 15; © Paule Seux/hemis.fr/Getty Images, p. 16; Private Collection/The Bridgeman Art Library, p. 18; © STR/AFP/Getty Images, p. 20; © age fotostock/SuperStock, pp. 21, 22, 66; © Win Initiative/Photodisc/Getty Images, p. 23 (main); © Richard I'Anson/Lonely Planet Images/Getty Images, p. 23 (inset); © Jeremy Richards/Dreamstime.com, p. 25; © Christophe Villedieu/Dreamstime.com, p. 26; Library of Congress, pp. 29 (LC–DIG–ggbain–32749), 34 (LC–USZ62–24984), 39 (LC-USZ62–123683); © Three Lions/Hulton Archive/Getty Images, p. 30; Keystone/Eyedea/Everett Collection, p. 31; © FPG/Hulton Archive/Getty Images, p. 32 (main); Mary Evans Picture Library/Everett Collection, pp. 32 (inset), 33; © Richard Passmore/Stone/Getty Images, p. 35; © iStockphoto.com/Paul Velgos, p. 36; © Lake County Museum/Curt Teich Postcard Archives/Hulton Archive/Getty Images, p. 40; © Adambooth/Dreamstime.com, p. 40; © Bettmann/CORBIS, pp. 43, 49; © Chris Pritchard/Photodisc/Getty Images, p. 44; © Scott Olson/Getty Images, p. 45; © DEA/G. COZZI/Getty Images, p. 46; © Hulton-Deutsch Collection/CORBIS, pp. 48, 51; © Eric Sierins/CORBIS, p. 50; © Tony Arruza/CORBIS, p. 52; © Marcus Vetter/CORBIS, p. 53; © TG Stock/Tim Graham Photo Library/Getty Images, p. 54; AP Photo/Russell McPhedran, p. 55; © Travel Ink/Gallo Images/Getty Images, pp. 56, 73 (center left); © Renaud Visage/Photographer's Choice RF/Getty Images, p. 58; © Gamma/Eyedea/ZUMA Press, p. 59; © Blueximages/Dreamstime.com, p. 60; © Ian Cumming/Axiom Photographic Agency/Getty Images, p. 61 (left); © Chris Jackson/Getty Images, p. 61 (right); © epa/CORBIS, p. 62; © Martha Camarillo/Reportage/Getty Images, p. 63; © Holger Mette/Dreamstime.com, p. 64; © Louie Psihoyos/CORBIS, p. 67; AP Photo/Chiang Ying-ying, p. 68; © Colin Galloway/Alamy, p. 69; © Kayte Deioma/Alamy, p. 70 (top); AP Photo/Jerome Favre, p. 70 (bottom); © Chien Ping Tsai/Dreamstime.com, p. 71; © Guy Vanderelst/Photographer's Choice RF/Getty Images, p. 73 (top center); © Amanda Hall/Robert Harding World Imagery/Getty Images, p. 73 (top right); © Sjakie123/Dreamstime.com, p. 73 (center right); © Michele Falzone/Photographer's Choice/Getty Images, p. 73 (bottom left); © Toyohiro Yamada/Taxi/Getty Images, p. 73 (bottom center); © Tim Graham/The Image Bank/Getty Images, p. 73 (bottom right).

Cover: © Amanda Hall/Robert Harding World Imagery/Getty Images (top left); © Guy Vanderelst/Photographer's Choice RF/Getty Images (top center); © Sjakie123/Dreamstime.com (top right); © Tim Graham/The Image Bank/Getty Images (center); © Michele Falzone/Photographer's Choice/Getty Images (bottom left); © Toyohiro Yamada/Taxi/Getty Images (bottom center); © Travel Ink/Gallo Images/Getty Images (bottom right).